He's crouched like a cat behind the big, old tractor tire that used to be a swing—before the rope rotted and fell from the branch of the oak tree.

He listens. He hears the girl's footsteps near the garden, on the driveway, now by the flowers along the walk.

She's getting closer.

Suddenly, there's another sound. A droning buzz.

The boy's hand flutters across his face and brushes the back of his neck.

Something else is looking for the boy.

This rose petal is splashed with dewdrops.

x1,140

5

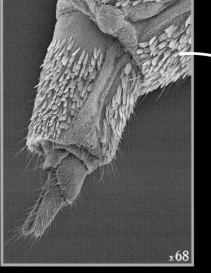

x68

The female *Culex* releases her eggs from a structure at the tip of her abdomen called an ovipositor.

Culex pipiens is the scientific name for the common house mosquito.

wings

abdomen

thorax

eye

palps →

legs

proboscis

antenn

x18

x330

A mosquito wing has feathery scales along its edges and veins, and hairs called setae on its surface.

6

capped with a rounded lens.

x370

Her name is *Culex pipiens*. Bordered with scales, her wings whine, beating about 500 times in one second. Her antennae, feathery and fine, detect the boy's breath. Her compound eyes guide her toward the boy's moving hand.

She's getting closer.

But this is not a playful game of hide-and-seek. *Culex* carries hundreds of tiny eggs inside her body. Finding the boy is a matter of life and death.

x145

This is a female mosquito antenna. *Culex*'s two antennae detect carbon dioxide, odors, heat, and humidity—all signals that lead her to blood.

Culex is a very young mosquito, yet already she's lived a dangerous and complicated life.

She started out as a tiny egg laid on the surface of the rainwater trapped inside the rim of the old tire.

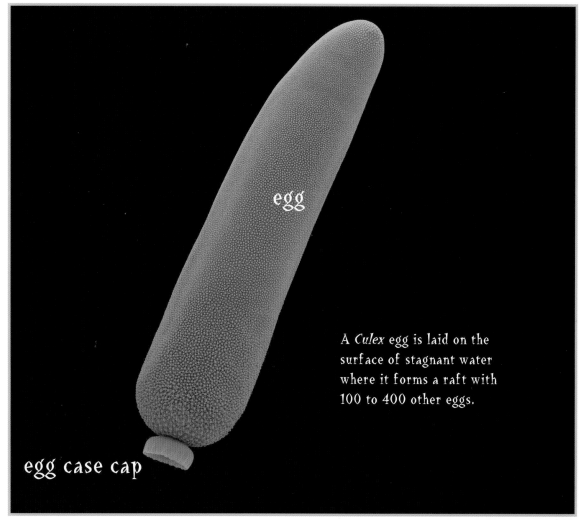

egg

egg case cap

A *Culex* egg is laid on the surface of stagnant water where it forms a raft with 100 to 400 other eggs.

x140

Attached to hundreds of other eggs, she
floated within an egg raft that was no
bigger than half a grain of rice.

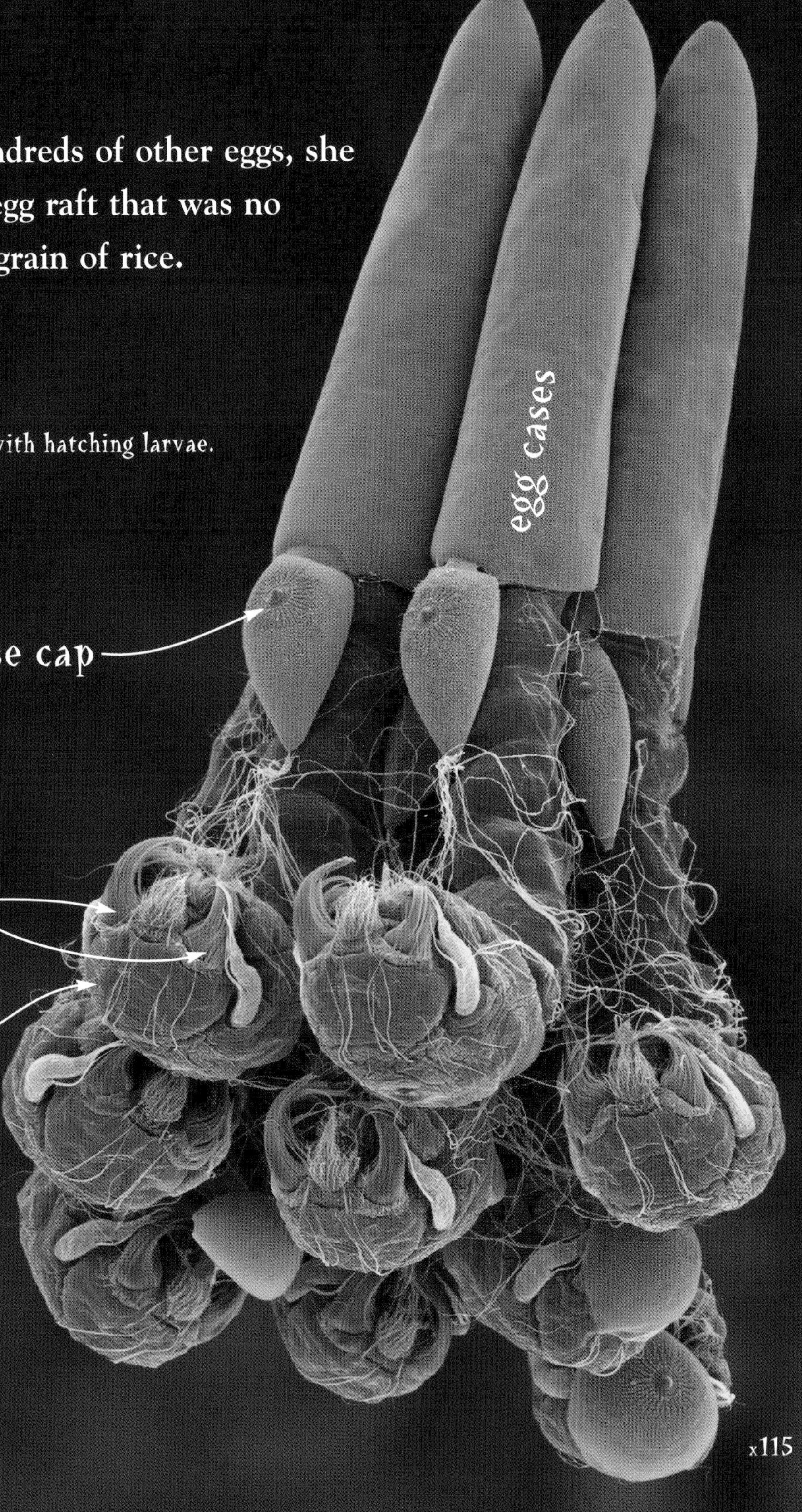

Part of an egg raft with hatching larvae.

egg cases

egg case cap

mouth
brushes

developing eye

x115

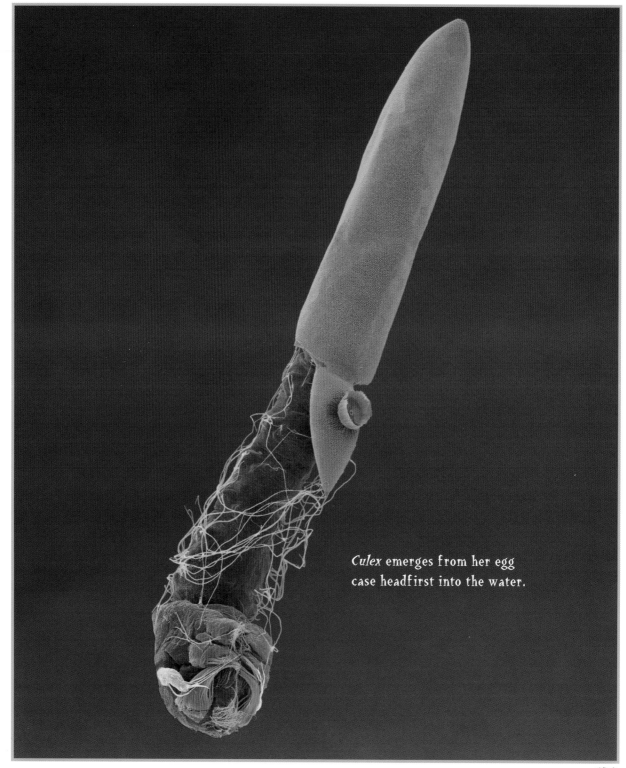

Culex emerges from her egg
case headfirst into the water.

10

x130

Two days later all the eggs hatched. *Culex* burst out of her shell—a long, wiggling worm. She had big eyes and a hairy head that hung down into the water. She breathed through a tube in her tail, called a siphon.

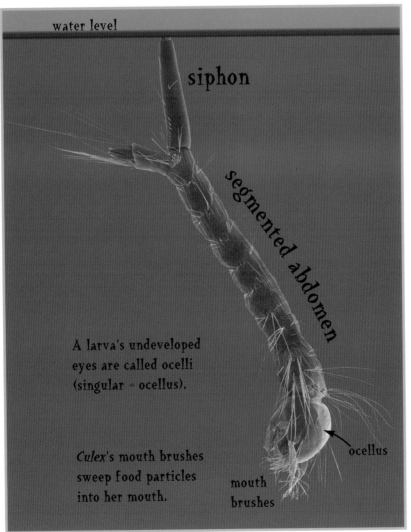

water level

siphon

segmented abdomen

A larva's undeveloped eyes are called ocelli (singular = ocellus).

Culex's mouth brushes sweep food particles into her mouth.

mouth brushes

ocellus

x22

11

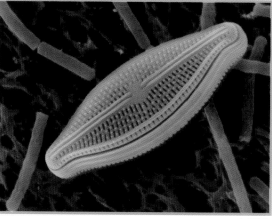

Culex feeds on plankton such as diatoms, which are single-celled algae with silica shells (shown in pink), and bacteria (orange rods). Some types of rod-shaped bacteria are deadly to mosquito larvae.

x1,830

For one week *Culex* fed on tiny creatures that also lived in the water. Day and night her waving whiskers swept the microscopic food into her open mouth.

All of *Culex*'s brothers and sisters fed in this manner, but not all of them lived. Some died from eating bacteria that cause disease. *Culex* was lucky. She survived and grew until she was three times her original size.

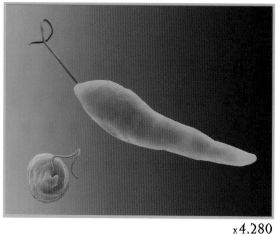

Euglena gracilis are another kind of plankton. They swim by whipping their thread-like flagellum.

x4,280

12

Some plankton, such as
Cyanobacteria, live near the
water's surface. They use energy
from sunlight to produce food in
a process called photosynthesis.

x1,955

These are other types
of diatoms.

x2,455

eye

antenna

antenna

palps

proboscis

labial sheath

labial sheath

knives

cutter

cutter

x4

x39

Culex feeds with the part of her mouth called the proboscis. Inside the proboscis is a pair of flexible serrated cutters that slide up and down alongside another pair of carving knives that slice through inner layers of skin.

A long pair of tubes is also found in the proboscis: one drips saliva into the wound, which keeps the blood flowing; the other is a straw for sucking in blood.

Culex is very close. She lands. She is so light the boy feels nothing. *Culex* pushes the tip of her mouth through the boy's skin. Her mouth is a bundle of long tubes and cutters that slide side by side like tiny knives.

The boy feels nothing.

Keeping her mouth in the hole, *Culex* stabs. With each poke, she pumps saliva from a tiny tube in her mouth. The saliva contains a chemical that will keep the blood flowing . . . if she ever finds it.

The boy feels nothing.

Finally, after fourteen stabs, *Culex* nicks a blood vessel. She tastes the blood. She immediately sucks a drop into her miniature straw. Now the blood is flowing, drop by drop, into her stomach.

Still the boy feels nothing.

Culex's belly swells. She is full.

At last the boy feels it: a mosquito bite!
As *Culex* struggles to lift her bloated body
into the thick night air, the boy smacks the back
of his neck.

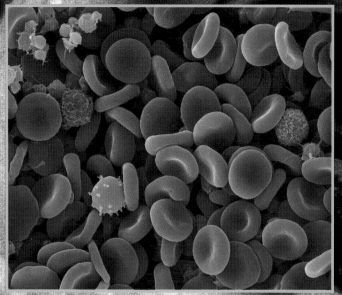

x1,530

Human blood contains red
blood cells (red) for carrying
oxygen, white blood cells
(green and purple) for
fighting infection, and
platelets (brown) for clotting.

"Found you!" shouts the girl. "Now you're 'it.'"

"And it's *your* turn to hide," says the boy.

Culex clings to the side of the big oak tree. Pink liquid containing the waste left over from her meal trickles from her body. It drips for almost an hour before *Culex* is light enough to fly.

That night in bed the boy scratches the itchy, hard, red lump that has appeared on the back of his neck. Hidden in darkness outside, *Culex* rests.

Tomorrow—and the next day, and the day after that—it will be *Culex*'s turn to hide. Spiders, insects, bats, and birds will hunt her until she is ready to lay her eggs . . .

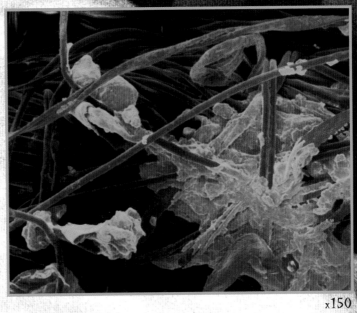

Flakes of dead skin (green) are tangled in the cotton fibers (blue) of the T-shirt.

x150

. . . on the surface of the rainwater trapped in the rim of the big, old tractor tire that used to be a swing—before the rope rotted and fell from the branch of the oak tree.

More About Mosquitoes

Mosquitoes lived amid the dinosaurs, feeding off their blood. Today *Culex pipiens* (the scientific name for the common house mosquito) prefers bird blood but also feeds on human blood. *Culex* thrives worldwide, wherever there is dirty, stagnant water and a blood supply.

Culex pipiens is just one of more than 2,700 mosquito species. Mosquitoes are found on every continent except Antarctica.

All mosquitoes need water in which to lay their eggs. Ponds, puddles, ditches, birdbaths, barrels, tree holes, and old tires provide a place for mosquito eggs to hatch and the larvae to grow.

Like butterflies, most mosquitoes feed on flower nectar and plant juices. Only the females of some species feed on blood to nourish their eggs. Fewer still feed mainly on human blood. Yet just one bite from an infected mosquito can cause illness. Although its name simply means "little fly" in Spanish, the mosquito is the deadliest animal on Earth.

Culex's Life Cycle

EGG: 1–2 days

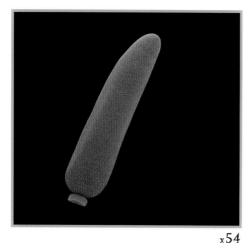

x54

WIGGLER (larva): 7–14 days

x9